IN FOCUS...
BASKETBALL

DENNIS PERNU

Quarto is the authority on a wide range of topics.

Quarto educates, entertains and enriches the lives of our readers—enthusiasts and lovers of hands-on living.

www.quartoknows.com

This library edition published in 2019
by Quarto Library,
an imprint of The Quarto Group.
6 Orchard Road
Suite 100
Lake Forest, CA 92630
T: +1 949 380 7510
F: +1 949 380 7575
www.QuartoKnows.com

Distributed in the United States and Canada by
Lerner Publisher Services
241 First Avenue North
Minneapolis, MN 55401 U.S.A.
www.lernerbooks.com

A CIP record for this book is available from the Library of Congress.

ISBN 978 0 7112 4797 0

Manufactured in Guangdong, China CC072019

9 8 7 6 5 4 3 2 1

MIX
Paper from
responsible sources
FSC® C008047

CONTENTS

Words in **bold** are explained in the Glossary on page 31

THE HISTORY
OF BASKETBALL

Basketball is a popular summertime playground sport. Most basketball leagues, however, hold their seasons during the winter months. This goes back all the way to the invention of basketball.

WOW!
The first basketball game was played on January 20, 1892. The final score? 1-0!

A Cold Start

Dr. James Naismith was a **physical education** professor in Springfield, Massachusetts. Naismith came up with an indoor game to keep his students active during the long, cold winters. In December 1891 he nailed two peach baskets to the balcony that circled the school's gymnasium. Teams tried to toss a soccer ball into the opposing team's peach basket. Naismith called his new game "basket ball."

Naismith was photographed with his first basketball team in 1891.

STAR PROFILE
JAMES NAISMITH

Born: November 6, 1861
Ontario, Canada
Died: November 28, 1939

Team Coached: University of Kansas

Star Stat: Incredibly, Naismith had a losing record (55 wins, 60 losses) as head basketball coach at the University of Kansas!

Changing the Game

At first, each team had nine players. A few years later, Naismith reduced the teams to five players each. He also added backboards behind the baskets. He found fans in the balcony could reach down and knock away the opposing team's shots!

The US Basketball Hall of Fame is located in Springfield, Massachusetts, in honor of James Naismith.

TIPOFF

Basketball is played on a court. Most basketball courts are inside gymnasiums and arenas and have wood floors. But basketball courts can also be found outdoors in parks and schoolyards, where they have asphalt, concrete, or even dirt surfaces.

The basket's rim is 10 feet (3.05 meters) above the floor. Still, many players are able to dunk the ball.

Hardwood and Hoops

College and pro courts are 94 feet (28.6 meters) long and 50 feet (15.2 meters) wide. Younger teams play on smaller courts. The court's floor is made of hard, polished wood. At each end there is a circular rim with a net called a basket. The rim is 10 feet (3 meters) above the court, so tall athletes often excel at basketball.

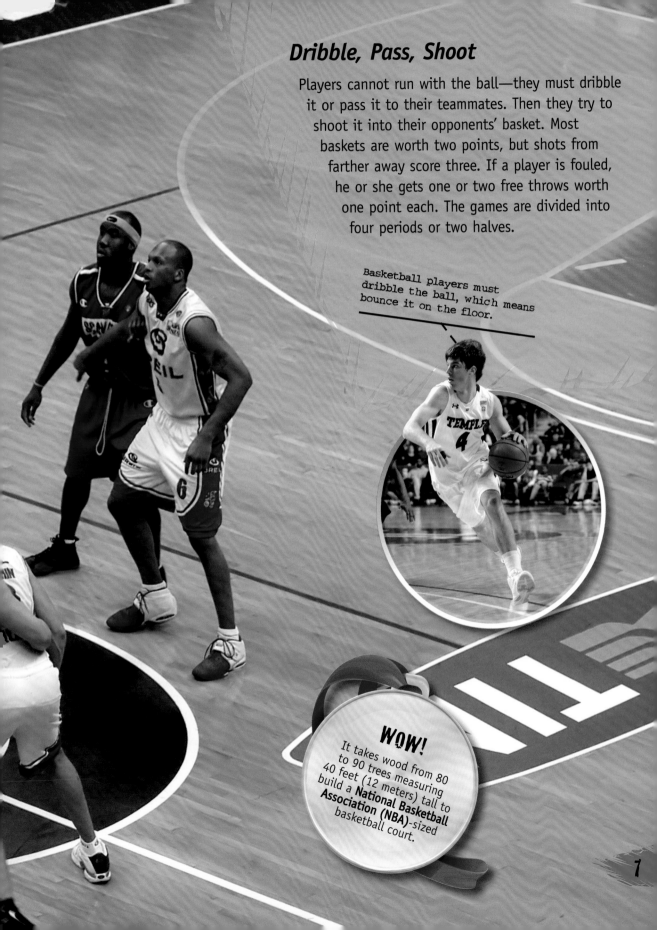

Dribble, Pass, Shoot

Players cannot run with the ball—they must dribble it or pass it to their teammates. Then they try to shoot it into their opponents' basket. Most baskets are worth two points, but shots from farther away score three. If a player is fouled, he or she gets one or two free throws worth one point each. The games are divided into four periods or two halves.

Basketball players must dribble the ball, which means bounce it on the floor.

WOW!

It takes wood from 80 to 90 trees measuring 40 feet (12 meters) tall to build a **National Basketball Association (NBA)**-sized basketball court.

BASKETBALL EQUIPMENT

Basketball's popularity has spread around the world. One reason is the equipment—you don't need a lot of it to enjoy the sport. A lot of parks have outdoor courts. And many gyms offer **pickup** games. All you need are a pair of sneakers and a friend with a ball.

Perfectly Round

"Roundball" is a slang term for the sport of basketball. That's because a basketball is shaped like a perfect sphere. It's about 30 inches (76 centimeters) around and usually orange in color with black lines, or ribs. Balls with a leather covering are best for indoor games. For playing outdoors, it's better to use one made of a tough material such as rubber. Dribbling a leather ball on asphalt can quickly ruin it.

The black lines on a basketball are called its ribs. This is a tough, outdoor ball.

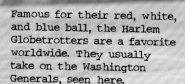
Famous for their red, white, and blue ball, the Harlem Globetrotters are a favorite worldwide. They usually take on the Washington Generals, seen here.

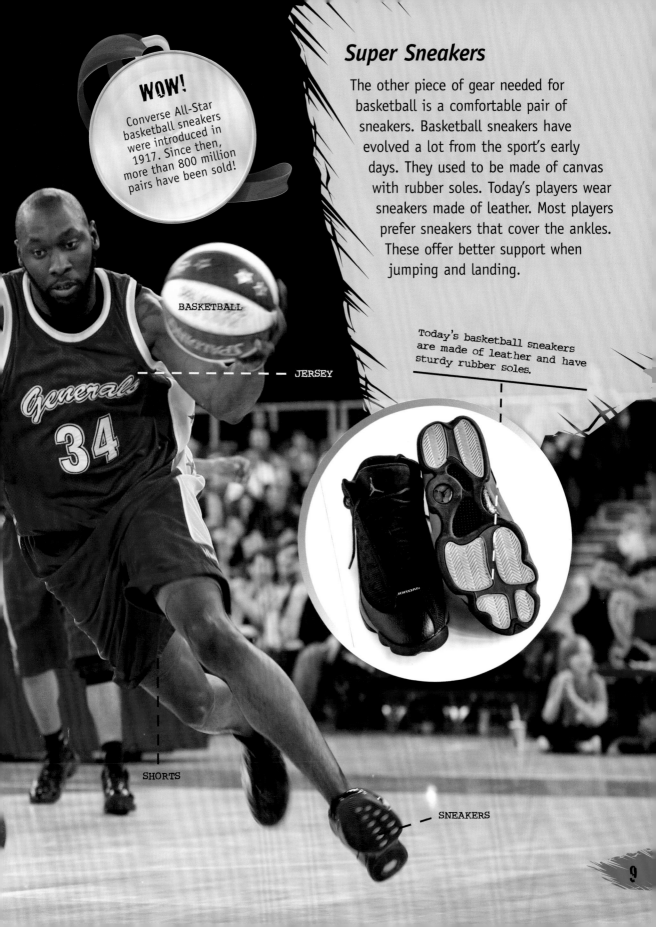

Super Sneakers

The other piece of gear needed for basketball is a comfortable pair of sneakers. Basketball sneakers have evolved a lot from the sport's early days. They used to be made of canvas with rubber soles. Today's players wear sneakers made of leather. Most players prefer sneakers that cover the ankles. These offer better support when jumping and landing.

Today's basketball sneakers are made of leather and have sturdy rubber soles.

BASKETBALL

JERSEY

34

SHORTS

SNEAKERS

THE CENTER

A basketball team has five players on the court. They work together on offense to score baskets. When their opponents have the ball, they play defense and try to prevent them from making baskets. One of the five players is the center, sometimes called the "big man" in the NBA.

Kevin McHale played both center and forward for the Boston Celtics.

Middle of the Action

The center is often a team's tallest player. On defense, the center usually hangs around his or her team's basket. When the other team misses a shot, the center tries to get the **rebound**. The center may also block shots. On offense, the center plays near the other team's basket. He or she battles for offensive rebounds and takes short shots. Occasionally the center makes a **slam dunk**, too.

WOW!
Centers Manute Bol and Gheorghe Muresan were the NBA's tallest players to date. Both stood 7 feet, 7 inches (2.3 meters) tall.

Some fans believe
Andre Drummond (#0)
of the Detroit
Pistons is the NBA's
best center.

NBA Big Men

George Mikan was the NBA's
first big man. He played for the
Minneapolis Lakers in the 1950s.
Many centers followed in his
footsteps. Wilt Chamberlain played
from 1959 to 1973 and still holds
the NBA record for most
rebounds (23,924). But his
greatest record is scoring 100
points in one game! Shaquille
O'Neal, another great center,
scored at least 20 points and
made 10 rebounds per game.

Wilt Chamberlain's
most remarkable
record is scoring
100 points in a
single game.

THE POWER FORWARD

There are two forward positions in basketball: power forward and small forward. Some of their jobs, like rebounding and blocking shots, overlap with the center's jobs. And like everyone on the team, they must pitch in on both offense and defense.

Forward Rebekkah Brunson dribbles the ball toward the basket in a European league game.

WOW!

Kevin Garnett has topped 25,000 points, 10,000 rebounds, 5,000 **assists**, 1,500 **steals**, and 1,500 blocked shots in his career—the only NBA player so far to do so.

Milwaukee Bucks' power forward Giannis Antetokounmpo leads his team at the Antetokounbros Streetball Event in Athens, Greece, in 2016.

Power Up

On offense, a power forward plays near the basket, watching his or her teammates. If a teammate shoots, the power forward knows to be ready for an offensive rebound. On defense, the power forward might play under his or her basket and help their team scoop up defensive rebounds. If their team plays a man-to-man defense, they cover one of the other team's forwards instead.

Power Players

Karl Malone helped define the power forward position. Malone was known as "the Mailman," because it was said he always delivered. He holds the record for second most career points (36,928). Charles ("Sir Charles") Barkley was another impressive power forward, effective at scoring and rebounding. Today, one of the best young power forwards is Giannis Antetokounmpo of the Milwaukee Bucks.

STAR PROFILE
TIM DUNCAN

Born: April 25, 1976
Christiansted,
US Virgin Islands

Team: San Antonio Spurs

Star Stats: 5x NBA champ, one of two players to win NBA championship in three decades (1990s, 2000s, 2010s)

Power forward Dirk Nowitzki played 21 seasons with the Dallas Mavericks. He led his team to 15 NBA playoffs.

13

THE SMALL FORWARD

Basketball's other forward position is small forward. Like their name suggests, small forwards usually aren't as big as power forwards. That's because their role is a bit different. It requires a little more speed than the power forward position.

A Bit of Everything

Often, the small forward can be seen dribbling the ball toward the opponent's basket. The small forward is also a good passer, giving the ball to teammates when he or she doesn't have a good scoring chance. When they do shoot, they tend to take most of their shots from farther out than the center. Small forwards also get rebounds if they can. In other words, they do a bit of everything.

WOW!

Small forward Alex English led the NBA in scoring during the 1980s with 19,682 points—despite never winning a league championship.

LeBron James is the premier small forward in basketball today.

Small forward Kevin Durant is one of the brightest stars in the NBA today.

14

Famous Forwards

Two of basketball's greatest players were considered small forwards. Julius "Dr. J" Erving played 17 pro seasons and was famous for his high-flying slam dunks. Larry Bird was less flashy, but helped the Boston Celtics win three championships in the 1980s. He later coached the Indiana Pacers. Today, the game's biggest star often plays small forward. LeBron James has been on three championship teams and is a four-time NBA MVP. And he went straight from high school to the pros!

STAR PROFILE
LARRY BIRD

Born: December 7, 1956
West Baden, Indiana

Team: Boston Celtics

Star Stats: 3x NBA champ,
3x NBA MVP

Julius "Dr. J" Erving was an electrifying player. As a forward, his style of play inspired an entire generation of players who followed.

GUARDS

There are two guards on the basketball court: a point guard and a shooting guard. But don't let their small size fool you—these players are critical to the teams. Point guards have recorded some of the most impressive statistics in basketball history.

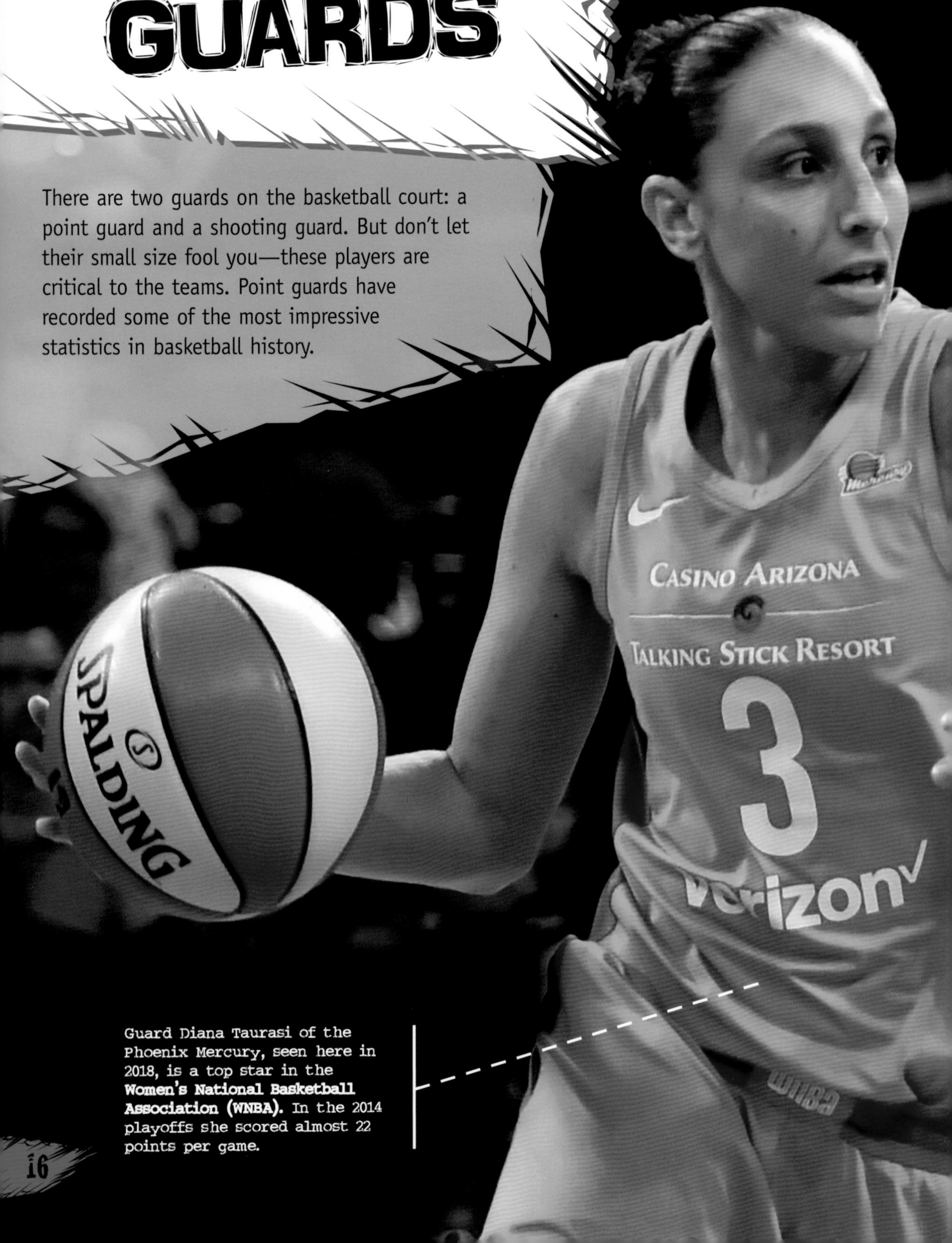

Guard Diana Taurasi of the Phoenix Mercury, seen here in 2018, is a top star in the **Women's National Basketball Association (WNBA).** In the 2014 playoffs she scored almost 22 points per game.

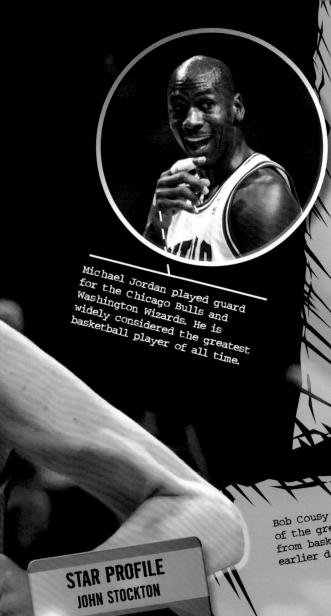

Like Mike

Guards are a team's best shooters and passers. They take a lot of shots from outside the **key**. A guard also helps run the team on the floor, much like a quarterback. They are often big stars. Michael Jordan, perhaps the NBA's greatest player of all time, was a shooting guard. Jordan led the Chicago Bulls to six championships. He also holds the NBA record for the highest points-per-game average (30.12).

Michael Jordan played guard for the Chicago Bulls and Washington Wizards. He is widely considered the greatest basketball player of all time.

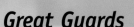

Bob Cousy was one of the great guards from basketball's earlier days.

STAR PROFILE
JOHN STOCKTON

Born: March 26, 1962
Spokane, Washington

Team: Utah Jazz

Star Stats: 15,806 career assists, 3,265 career steals (both NBA records)

Great Guards

Just as George Mikan revolutionized the center position, Bob Cousy did the same for guards. He set many assist records and was known for his quick style of play. Earvin "Magic" Johnson was another great point guard. He helped the Lakers to five championships and set playoff assist records in the process. More recently, John Stockton showed what a speedy guard can do for his team, setting career assist and steal records.

17

THE COACH

It takes work to be a good basketball team. The players do their part to improve, and the coach is there to help them. A head coach has a big part in a team's success. No wonder some coaches get almost as much attention as their players.

WOW!

Lenny Wilkens coached six teams in 2,487 NBA games over 32 seasons. Of those games, a total of 1,412 were wins for his teams.

Coach Pat Summitt explains a play to her team in 2011. Most basketball coaches use a dry-erase board like this during games.

Big Job

A basketball coach has many tasks. He or she prepares the team for its next opponent. This means learning the opponent's strengths and weaknesses. During the game the coach sends in **subs** who best match up against opposing players. The coach even makes sure players are in top shape for long games. The coach usually has one or two assistants to help with all these tasks.

Coach Phil Jackson argues a call with a referee during a game in 2006. Jackson is one of the most successful NBA coaches of all time.

Basketball Brains

John Wooden achieved a coaching record with his UCLA team—it won seven NCAA championships in a row (1967–1973). Pat Summitt was also a great coach. She won eight out of every ten games she coached! Another superstar coach is Mike Krzyzewski (pronounced she-SHEV-ski) of Duke University, who had won 1,059 games through the 2018–2019 season. At the pro level, perhaps the greatest coach ever was Phil Jackson. His teams won 11 NBA championships.

In addition to coaching Duke University, Coach Mike Krzyzewski led the USA Olympic basketball team in 2008 and 2012.

THE WNBA

In 1997 a new pro sports league began play in the United States. The Women's National Basketball Association (WNBA) was formed with eight teams. It gives players from women's college basketball a chance to extend their playing careers. It also gives fans exciting basketball action.

Maya Moore of the Minnesota Lynx takes a shot against the Phoenix Mercury.

Sue Bird of the Seattle Storm prepares to pass an orange and white WNBA ball.

WNBA Basics

The WNBA season is held from May to October and lasts 34 games plus playoffs. Game rules are mostly the same as those used in the NBA. One difference is that each quarter is 10 minutes long instead of 12. Since 1997, the league has grown to 12 teams. In addition, WNBA players represent more than 20 nations.

Sheryl Swoopes was the first player to sign a contract to play in the WNBA. She was named league MVP three times and played 12 seasons in the WNBA.

Leading Ladies

Though not even 20 years old, the WNBA has produced many star players. Two of the greatest entered the league in its first season: Sheryl Swoopes and Tina Thompson. Both were members of four championship teams. Thompson played 15 seasons. One of today's most exciting younger players is Maya Moore. Maya has helped her Minnesota Lynx to two WNBA titles.

STAR PROFILE
TINA THOMPSON

Born: February 10, 1975 Los Angeles, California

Teams: Houston Comets, Los Angeles Sparks, Seattle Storm

Star Stats: 7,488 career points, 16,088 minutes played (both WNBA records), 4x WNBA champion

WOW!
On June 2, 2012, Angel McCoughtry of the Atlanta Dream made 17 out of 17 free throw attempts against the Chicago Sky, missing none!

MARCH MADNESS

Every spring, basketball fans have something big to cheer about. It's tournament time! The National Collegiate Athletic Association (NCAA) chooses the college teams that will play in the NCAA Tournament. It's the biggest sports story of the month and it's known as "March Madness."

Lew Alcindor led the UCLA Bruins to three NCAA tournaments (1967–1969).

Bracket Basics

Sixty-eight teams are picked to play in the tournament. The teams are placed in a four-part **bracket** and ranked from strongest to weakest. Stronger teams play weaker teams in the first round of games. This is where much of the tournament's excitement comes into play. Every year, some weaker teams upset stronger teams. Before the tournament begins, fans try to predict who will win each game.

STAR PROFILE
CHRISTIAN LAETTNER

Born: August 17, 1969
Angola, New York

Team: Duke University

Star Stats: 407 points, 23 games played (both NCAA Tournament records)

The NCAA Final Four often takes place in football stadiums to hold the huge crowds.

An NCAA Tournament bracket has a space for each team. Winners advance to the next round in the bracket until only two teams remain.

From 68 Down to 1

The NCAA Tournament takes more than two weeks to play. With each round, the number of teams decreases by half. The last three rounds are known as the Sweet Sixteen, the Elite Eight, and the Final Four. The Final Four is played at a **neutral site**. The NCAA also hosts a tournament for its women's teams. The women's event begins with 64 teams.

NBA CHAMPIONSHIP

A few weeks after March Madness, the pros begin their own tournament: the NBA Playoffs. The NBA is considered the world's top basketball league. In the playoffs, the season's best teams compete.

The winning team in the NBA Finals is awarded the Larry O'Brien Championship Trophy. It is covered in 24-karat gold.

How It Works

The 16 NBA teams with the best regular-season records get to play in the **postseason.** The playoffs begin with four best-of-seven series. The first team in each series to win four games moves on to play a new opponent.

Stephen Curry (#30) of the Golden State Warriors drives to the basket against the Portland Trail Blazers in the NBA Western Conference Finals in 2019.

WOW!

The Boston Celtics have won the most NBA Championships (17).

Dynasties

Some teams have enjoyed great playoff success. These teams are known as **dynasties**. The Boston Celtics and Los Angeles Lakers have had the NBA's most famous dynasties. Other top teams include the Chicago Bulls (1991–1998), Miami Heat (2011–2014), and San Antonio Spurs (1999–2014).

STAR PROFILE
JOE MONTANA

Born: February 12, 1934 West Monroe, Louisiana

Team: Boston Celtics

Star Stats: 11x NBA champion (NBA record)

Scottie Pippen was a small forward who helped the Chicago Bulls win six NBA championships in the 1990s.

Playoff Performers

Every dynasty is powered by great players. Michael Jordan and Scottie Pippen led the Chicago Bulls to six titles in the 1990s. But the player with the most NBA championships is Bill Russell.

25

ALL-STAR GAME

In February, the NBA's season reaches its halfway point. Most NBA players get a short break from their games while others play in the league's All-Star Game. The NBA's top stars aren't the only players honored with this special game—the WNBA has an All-Star Game, too.

The coaches with the best regular season records are named the coaches of the All Star Game.

Choosing Sides

The first NBA All-Star Game was played in 1951 in Boston, Massachusetts. Today, fans, sportswriters, and the players themselves vote for the **starters** in the All-Star Game. The coaches and two team captains choose the rest of their teams. There is one team for the Western Conference and one for the Eastern Conference. Each team has 14 players.

All-Star Weekends

All-star games are celebrations of the sports and their athletes. In addition to the All-Star Games, NBA and WNBA players test their basketball skills. In the WNBA Three-Point Shootout, players try to make as many **three-pointers** as they can in one minute. The Slam Dunk Contest is one of the most popular events of the NBA All-Star Weekend. Players are scored on their ability to perform high-flying dunks.

WOW!
The NBA All-Star ballot is offered in three languages: English, Spanish, and Chinese.

Sue Bird has appeared in more WNBA All Star Games than any other player.

STAR PROFILE
Earvin "Magic" Johnson

Born: August 14, 1959 Lansing, Michigan

Team: Los Angeles Lakers

Star Stats: 127 All-Star Game assists (NBA record)

27

SHOOTIN' HOOPS

College and pro basketball players are among the world's most amazing athletes. All of them learned their skills in places like small-town gymnasiums and big-city playgrounds. You can find people of all ages and abilities learning and enjoying basketball across the country.

WOW!

New York City must be the greatest city for streetball. It has nearly 600 parks with outdoor basketball courts.

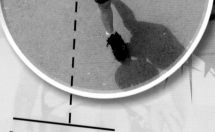

Outdoor parks are a great place to sharpen your basketball skills.

Youth Leagues

Most players learn basketball rules and skills in youth leagues. These are found at schools, parks, and churches. Often, youth games are played on half courts with lowered nets. This increases scoring chances for younger (and shorter!) players. It also means two games can be played on one court.

Streetball

Public parts are another place to learn basketball. This is sometimes called "streetball" because the courts are outdoors and made of asphalt, just like a street. Older, more skilled players can also be found playing at parks. Some of the best NBA players learned the game and sharpened their skills here.

Streetball tournaments can attract great **amateur** players.

More than 100,000 people around the world compete in wheelchair basketball. It can be played outdoors or on a standard court.

Friends play a game of one-on-one at an outdoor park. Nearly every town and city in the USA has at least one park with a **backboard** and net.

Get Out and Play

One of the best things about basketball is that just two people can play. Grab a friend at the park for a game of **horse** or **one-on-one**. Both are fantastic ways to practice dribbling and shooting—and to get exercise and hang out with a friend!

29

CREDITS

AUTHOR'S NOTE

I hope you have enjoyed reading all about the history, rules, and superstars of basketball! Maybe you and your friends were even inspired to get outside and give basketball a try.

Over the years I have had the pleasure of writing books about many different topics, from hot rod cars to haunted houses, but sports have always been one of my favorite things to write (and read!) about. When I was a youngster in school, most of my reading time was spent learning about sports stars of years past. I was also lucky to participate in several sports, often at the encouragement of my parents, including ice hockey, baseball, tennis, football, golf, and even BMX racing. I was never the best among my peers in any of those sports, but it turns out that wasn't the point. I learned all about teamwork from some of my great coaches (like Lowell Thomas and Randy Reigstad), made lifelong friends, collected favorite memories, and got plenty of exercise!

Today I live in Minneapolis, Minnesota. It is known as the "City of Lakes" and it is a wonderful place to get outside and be active throughout the year. There's fishing, canoeing, bicycling, and swimming in the summer, and skating, sledding, and skiing during the long winters. The parks offer sports leagues for kids of all ages, and today I am lucky to pay forward the lessons I learned from those fantastic coaches of my youth by coaching my sons, Leo and Gus, and their ice hockey teams.

Keep reading, but keep moving, too!
Dennis Pernu

GLOSSARY

amateur
an athlete who is not paid to play his or her sport; the opposite of professional

assist
a point that's awarded to a player who passes the basketball to a teammate who then scores; assists are not recorded on the scoreboard

backboard
the large glass, steel, or wooden board to which a basketball net and hoop are attached

bracket
a diagram that shows the games that are to be played in a tournament

dynasty/dynasties
a team that wins several league championships in a row

horse
a game in which the winner is the player to make five basketball shots that his or her opponent then misses

key
the area of a basketball court from the end line beneath the net to the free-throw line; also called the "lane" and the "paint"

National Basketball Association (NBA)
a men's professional basketball league in North America composed of 30 teams

neutral site
a stadium that is not in the home city of either team playing in the game

one-on-one
informal game in which two basketball players compete against each other, usually on a half-court

physical education
the teaching of exercise, sports, and healthy habits; sometimes simply called "phys ed"

pickup
describes an informal game in which players show up and sides are chosen

postseason
the playoffs that occur after a sport's leagues' regular season

rebound
in basketball, the recovery of a missed shot that bounces off the backboard or rim

slam dunk
the jamming of a basketball through the rim

starter
player who begins a game

stats
numbers used in any sport to measure an athlete's performance

steal
a statistic awarded to a defensive player who forces a turnover by intercepting or deflecting a pass or a dribble of an offensive player

sub
a player sent into a game to relieve a tired teammate or to better match up against an opponent

three-pointers
successful shots that are awarded three points rather than two because of their greater distance from the hoop

Women's National Basketball Association (WNBA)
a women's professional basketball league in the United States, composed of 12 teams

INDEX